Sunshine & Shadow

Other For Better or For Worse® Collections

Middle Age Spread
Growing Like a Weed
Love Just Screws Everything Up
Starting from Scratch
"There Goes My Baby!"
Things Are Looking Up . . .
What, Me Pregnant?
If This Is a Lecture, How Long Will It Be?
Pushing 40
It's All Downhill from Here
Keep the Home Fries Burning
The Last Straw
Just One More Hug
"It Must Be Nice to Be Little"
Is This "One of Those Days," Daddy?
I've Got the One-More-Washload Blues . . .

Retrospectives

Remembering Farley: A Tribute to the Life of Our Favorite Cartoon Dog
It's the Thought that Counts . . . Fifteenth Anniversary Collection
A Look Inside . . . For Better or For Worse: The 10th Anniversary Collection

Sunshine & Shadow

A *For Better or For Worse*® Collection by Lynn Johnston

Andrews McMeel
Publishing

Kansas City

ISBN: 0-7407-0200-9

Library of Congress Catalog Card Number: 99-72693

For 3 years, our mother confronted and fought cancer with more stamina and resourcefulness than one could think possible.

During the latter part of her illness when we knew she would have to give in, we talked openly about her last journey; what would the experience be like? Who would she meet — and, because she had always been such a wonderful organizer, would she have to work when she got there? I asked her to watch over our children and they know she has done so, tirelessly.

She left us with the knowledge that such difficult times can be endured with courage, optimism, faith and a rich sense of humor.

This collection is dedicated to Ursula Marian Ridgway.

BEEP- BEEP!

ELIZABETH HAS BEEN USING YOUR CAR A LOT LATELY, EL.

I KNOW... BUT SHE'S CAREFUL WITH IT.

STILL, IT'S PRETTY GENEROUS OF YOU TO LET HER HAVE IT AGAIN TONIGHT.

OH, NOT REALLY.

-IT'S OUT OF GAS.

IT'S COOL OF YOUR MOM TO LET US USE HER CAR LIKE THIS, LIZ!

YEAH-SHE'S OK!

WHAT'S THE MELBORP?

THAT'S "PROBLEM" SPELLED BACKWARDS.

WHAT?

WE'RE SAYING STUFF BACKWARDS TONIGHT, AN' YOU'RE NOT WITH US!—WHAT'S THE MELBORP?

... WE'RE OUTTA SAG!

HOW MUCH GAS DO WE HAVE LEFT, ZIL?

ZIL! GET IT, LIZ? THAT'S YOUR NAME SAID BACKWARDS!

ENOUGH TO GET TO GORDON'S GARAGE—AND THANK GOODNESS IT'S UP AHEAD!

HEY, LOOK! OIL SAID BACKWARDS IS LIO!

PREMIUM IS MUIMERP!

SPARK PLUG IS KRAPS GULP!

HA HA HA

HI, NODROG! LLIF TI PU!

WHY ARE PEOPLE SELLING POPPIES TODAY, MOM?

THEY'RE A SYMBOL, APRIL. SOMETHING TO MAKE US REMEMBER.

A MAN CALLED JOHN McCRAE WROTE A BEAUTIFUL POEM ABOUT THE POPPIES THAT GREW IN FLANDERS FIELDS.

ALSO IN THE FIELDS WERE CROSSES, MARKING THE GRAVES OF SOLDIERS WHO DIED FIGHTING THE WAR.

WHY DO I HAFTA WEAR A POPPY?!

I'M NOT REALLY SURE WHAT A WAR IS!

I KNOW.

LEST WE FORGET

AND THAT, I THINK, IS THE BEST REASON OF ALL!

APRIL, I TOOK THE STOCKING OFF YOUR HEAD, SO QUIT SCRATCHING!

I CAN'T!

SOMETHING'S MAKING MY HEAD ITCH!

—LET ME SEE.

EEWWWWW! SOMETHING'S **IN** THERE!—I THINK IT'S HEAD LICE!!

UH?

NIAAAA!

I GOTS HEAD-LIGHTS!!

HEAD LICE? OH, NO! OH MY GOSH! HOW DID THIS HAPPEN?!!

I DON'T KNOW. WHAT IS IT?!!

YOU HAVE TINY BUGS LIVING IN YOUR HAIR, APRIL! I HAVE TO GO TO THE PHARMACY RIGHT AWAY AND GET SOME STUFF TO GET RID OF THEM!

DON'T WORRY, HONEY. THEY'RE HARMLESS. —THEY WON'T HURT YOU!...I'LL BE RIGHT BACK.

JUST DON'T TOUCH **ANYTHING!**

GET AWAY FROM ME, APRIL!

HOWCOME?

'CAUSE HEAD LICE CAN SPREAD TO OTHER PEOPLE! I DON'T WANNA CATCH WHAT YOU HAVE!—STAY AWAY!

RINGG

HELLO? UH, HI, ANTHONY....

OH, NOTHING. JUST BABY-SITTING MY LOUSY LITTLE SISTER.

12

MOM? HOW LONG DO I HAFTA SIT IN THE BAFTUB?

ANOTHER FIFTEEN MINUTES, APRIL.

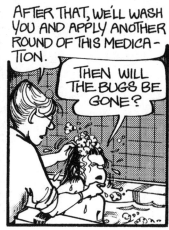

AFTER THAT, WE'LL WASH YOU AND APPLY ANOTHER ROUND OF THIS MEDICA-TION.

THEN WILL THE BUGS BE GONE?

NO. THEN WE HAVE TO BOIL OR PUT INTO PLASTIC BAGS ALL OF THE THINGS YOU TAKE TO BED WITH YOU.

CONNIE, DO YOU HAVE ANY LIQUID BLEACH?

SURE, EL.

WHAT'S THE HURRY?

I HAVE TO WASH ALL OF OUR SHEETS AND PILLOWCASES AND MATTRESS COVERS.

IS THERE SOME KIND OF PLAGUE AT YOUR HOUSE?

APRIL CAME HOME WITH HEAD LICE.

BLE

IT'S NOT **THAT** CONTA-GIOUS!!!

WHO WAS RUMMAGING THROUGH MY TOP DRAWER HERE?

UH...WE WERE.

WHAT ON EARTH FOR?

APRIL WANTED TO PUT A KNEE-HIGH ON HER HEAD.

SHE TOLD ME TO!!

SO, I GUESS SOMEBODY HASTA WASH ALL YOUR NYLONS, NOW... HUH?

WELL, LIZ...ISN'T IT NICE TO KNOW YOU'RE A "SOMEBODY"?!

13

I WASHED ALL OF THE CLOTHES APRIL HAS WORN FOR THE PAST 2 WEEKS, INCLUDING HATS, SCARVES COATS AND MITTENS.

WE'VE BOILED THE SHEETS AND PILLOWCASES, BAGGED PILLOWS AND TOYS, VACUUMED ALL THE RUGS AND MATTRESSES ... AND, WE'VE ALL BEEN CHECKED THOROUGHLY.

IS OUR HEAD LICE PROBLEM OVER?

I'M ABSOLUTELY POSITIVE.

GOOD!

SCRATCH ITCH SCRATCH ITCH ITCH SCRATCH! SCRATCH SCRATCH SCRATCH SCRATCH ITCH

SCRATCH SCRATCH SCRATCH ITCH SCRATCH ITCH ITCH SCRATCH ITCH SCRATCH ITCH ITCH, ITCH

MOM? HOWCOME I HAD BUGS IN MY HAIR?

WELL, IT SOME-TIMES HAPPENS WHEN CHILDREN ARE IN BIG GROUPS, APRIL. THEY USUALLY PASS FROM ONE PERSON TO ANOTHER.

HAVEN'T THEY TOLD YOU ABOUT THESE THINGS IN SCHOOL?

NOT YET.

—BUT THEY DID TEACH US HOW TO SHARE!

GUESS WHAT, APRIL!—AFTER YOUR MOM TOLD THE TEACHER YOU HAD HEAD LICE—LOTS MORE KIDS HAD IT, TOO!

THEY'RE CHECKING EVERYONE IN THE SCHOOL, AN' WE HAFTA TAKE THIS PAPER HOME, THAT EXPLAINS WHAT TO DO!

MORE KIDS GOT IT, DUNCAN?

UH-HUH. BUT I THINK YOU WERE THE FIRST.

REALLY? COOL!!

THIS IS THE FIRST TIME I'VE EVER BEEN FIRST IN ANYTHING!!

WHAT A BEAUTIFUL CLEAR NIGHT – ISN'T THAT THE NORTH STAR?

I'M NOT SURE!

IMAGINE, ANCIENT SEA-MEN... TRYING TO SAIL ACROSS THE OCEAN, WITH NOTHING BUT THE STARS TO GUIDE THEM.

HOW DID THEY FEEL WHEN THE SKY WAS OBSCURED AND THE SEA WAS ROUGH?

PROBABLY THE WAY I DO!

I WRITE MY BIG BIO-CHEMISTRY EXAM TOMORROW!

YOU'LL PASS THE EXAM TOMORROW, DEANNA. YOU'VE DONE WELL IN BIOCHEM ALL YEAR.

THERE'S JUST SO MUCH TO KNOW. IT'S SO EASY TO MAKE A MISTAKE, AND ONE TINY ERROR CAN COST YOU!

I THINK THE ANALOGY ABOUT SAILORS TRYING TO NAVIGATE IN A STORM JUST ABOUT DESCRIBES EXAM TIME.

YEAH...

...AND WE'RE ALL IN THE SAME BOAT!

WELL, I GUESS I'D BETTER GO.

ME, TOO.

GOODBYE.

'BYE.

....YOU FIRST.

MICHAEL, ARE YOU OK? YOU LOOK AWFUL!

THANK YOU.

WE SPENT ALL NIGHT GETTING THE CAMPUS PAPER OUT, AND I DIDN'T GET HOME UNTIL 5.

THEN I HAD STUFF TO READ AND AN EVALUATION TO PREPARE FOR...

THIS IS KILLING ME, DEANNA. I CAN'T **DO** THIS! I JUST CAN'T STAY AWAKE FOR 24 HOURS ANY-MORE!!

UNLESS, OF COURSE, THERE'S A PARTY.

HOW WAS YOUR EXAM THIS MORNING?

I PASSED, BUT I DON'T KNOW BY HOW MUCH.

AFTERWARDS, EVERYONE STOOD AROUND, COMPLAINING ABOUT THE QUESTIONS. SOME OF THEM WERE TOTALLY AMBIGUOUS!!

WHAT I WANT IS A STRAIGHTFORWARD QUESTION, TO WHICH I CAN GIVE A STRAIGHTFORWARD ANSWER!

OK.

...DO YOU LOVE ME?

MICHAEL, MY HEAD IS WHIRLING AROUND WITH MEDICAL TERMINOLOGY, BIOSTATISTICAL GRAPHING, PHARMACOLOGICAL CROSS-REFERENCING...

DEANNA... DO YOU LOVE ME? I'VE TOLD YOU THAT I LOVE YOU, BUT YOU'VE NEVER REALLY TOLD ME.

I'VE NEVER ACTUALLY HEARD THE WORDS.

I KNOW...

I GUESS I FIND THEM A LITTLE HARD TO SAY.

DEANNA, WE'VE BEEN DATING FOR A YEAR NOW... DO YOU LOVE ME?

YOU KNOW THE ANSWER TO THAT, MICHAEL. I MUST HAVE SHOWN YOU IN A THOUSAND WAYS!!

DEANNA. DO YOU LOVE ME?

I MUST—OR I WOULDN'T FEEL THE WAY I FEEL!

WHY ARE YOU ASKING ME THIS QUESTION WHEN WE'RE RIGHT IN THE MIDDLE OF EXAMS?

I DIDN'T THINK THE ANSWER WOULD BE MULTIPLE CHOICE.

I'M SORRY. I DIDN'T REALIZE YOU WERE SO UNSURE.

I'M NOT UNSURE ABOUT YOU. I'M UNSURE ABOUT ME.

MICHAEL, I ALMOST GOT MARRIED, REMEMBER? I TOLD HIM I LOVED HIM, AND I THOUGHT I MEANT IT THEN.

I DON'T WANT TO TELL ANYONE ELSE THAT I LOVE THEM UNTIL I KNOW, IN MY HEART, THAT IT'S ABSOLUTELY TRUE.

...DO YOU LIKE ME, THEN?

ABSOLUTELY.

19

WHAT'S HAPPENING?
I'M WORKING ON THE TEXT THAT GOES WITH YOUR PHOTO ESSAY.

BUT YOU'RE HUMMING. ONE DOESN'T HUM AFTER 2 HOURS' SLEEP AND A CHILI DOG. NOT VOCALLY, ANYWAY.

KNOW WHAT YOU NEED IN YOUR LIFE, JO? YOU NEED TO FALL IN LOVE. YOU NEED TO FIND A SINCERE, UNCOMPLICATED RELATIONSHIP.

I ALREADY HAVE, MAN!

SMAK

MAN, I WISH THESE GUYS WOULD GET A NEW ENLARGER. THIS ONE HAS TO BE 20 YEARS OLD!

WHAT ARE YOU DOING NOW?
DARKENING THE MAIN IMAGE A LITTLE.

YOU COULD DO ALL THIS ON A COMPUTER, WEED.
I KNOW.

BUT FOR ME, PHOTOGRAPHY IS LIKE A LOVE AFFAIR, MIKE.

IT'S BETTER WHEN EVERYTHING IS "HANDS ON."

HERE ARE THE WRITE-UPS TO GO WITH YOUR LAST SET OF PHOTOS, WEED.
HEY! LOOKIN' GOOD.
DARKROOM IN USE

I'M LEAVING TODAY WITH DEANNA.
OK—I'M GONNA STAY HERE, AN' WORK ON MY EXHIBIT.

JO…DON'T WORK TOO HARD, ALL RIGHT? GO HOME, YOU NEED A GOOD BREAK FROM SCHOOL.

FOR SOME OF US…. SCHOOL IS A GOOD BREAK FROM HOME!

21

I'M GOING TO OPEN THE WINDOW, O.K., DEANNA?

GOOD IDEA.

TURN THE HEATER OFF; THAT MIGHT HELP.

SURE.

MAYBE IF WE TURN UP THE FAN!

OR.... WE COULD PULL OVER AND PUT OUR LAUNDRY IN THE TRUNK.

LYNN

ELLY, WHY DO YOU KEEP LOOKING OUT THE WINDOW?

MICHAEL'S COMING HOME TONIGHT

WELL, STANDING THERE ISN'T GOING TO MAKE HIM COME HOME ANY FASTER.

I KNOW.

SO, STOP FIDGETING!

O.K.—IT'S JUST THAT HE'S BRINGING HIS NEW GIRLFRIEND WITH HIM.

LYNN

ARE YOU WORRIED ABOUT MEETING MY PARENTS, DEANNA?

A LITTLE.

I'M A LITTLE NERVOUS ABOUT MEETING YOUR MOTHER!

YOU SHOULDN'T BE—SHE'S O.K.

MICHAEL, SHE IS GOING TO LOOK AT ME AND ANALYZE ME AND WONDER IF I'M GOOD ENOUGH FOR HER SON!

WHAT'S THE POINT? I'VE DONE THAT ALREADY!

LYNN

CAN I HELP YOU WITH ANYTHING, MRS. PATTERSON?

PLEASE, CALL ME ELLY!

EVERYONE CALLS ME ELLY —ACTUALLY, I WAS NAMED FOR MY GRANDMOTHER, WHOSE NAME WAS ELIZABETH, BUT MY PARENTS CALLED ME ELLY....

AND MY BROTHER PHIL WAS NAMED FOR OUR AUNT PHYLLIS, WHO'S STILL IN ENGLAND, BUT YACK, YACK, YACK....

SO? WHAT'S SHE LIKE?

NICE GIRL, JOHN.... BUT AWFULLY QUIET.

SO, DEANNA—YOU AND MICHAEL HAVE KNOWN EACH OTHER FOR QUITE A WHILE!

WE MET IN GRADE SCHOOL, ACTUALLY.

AND YOU'RE STUDYING PHARMACY?

I HAVE ANOTHER YEAR TO GO BEFORE I GRADUATE.

YOUR FAMILY LIVES IN BURLINGTON?

UH·HUH. —MY MOM'S A NURSE AND MY DAD OWNS A HARDWARE STORE.

A **HARDWARE** STORE?

...YOU'RE IN.

WELL.... HOW DID I DO?

GREAT! THEY'RE CRAZY ABOUT YOU!

I'VE NEVER BEEN NERVOUS ABOUT MEETING SOMEONE'S FAMILY BEFORE.

YEAH... I WAS NERVOUS ABOUT MEETING YOUR FAMILY TOO

DUMB, ISN'T IT? LIKE, WE HAVEN'T ACTUALLY MADE A COMMITTMENT. I MEAN, WE'RE NOT EXACTLY SERIOUS OR ANYTHING.

NO....

NOT EXACTLY.

25

BEEP, BEEP, BOOP, FLADDAP!

BEEP BIP BOOP

MONEY
MONEY
MONEY
MONEY

LA, LA LA-LA LA!

IT ISN'T FREE, APRIL.—THIS REPRESENTS A LOT OF HARD WORK!

I KNOW.

WE MUSTA BEEN IN LINE FOR AN **HOUR**!!

ISN'T CHRISTMAS EVE GREAT, MOM?

YES...

—IT'S THE ONLY TIME I SEE YOU PEOPLE HANG SOMETHING UP!

LOOK, APRIL, LOOK! SANTA CAME!

SANTA WAS HERE! SEE? HE CAME LAST NIGHT!

QUICK! LOOK! SEE WHAT HE BROUGHT YOU!!!

IT'S SO COOL TO WATCH LITTLE KIDS ON CHRISTMAS MORNING. —THEY GET SO EXCITED!

URRBPPP!

Chocolates

JOHN!

—WHERE ARE YOU GOING WITH THAT?

IT'S USED PAPER. I'M GOING TO RECYCLE IT.

WHAT?

YOU KNOW I LIKE TO KEEP THE CHRISTMAS WRAP!

SEE? IT'S ALL CAREFULLY SMOOTHED AND FOLDED.

ELLY, YOU'RE NEVER GOING TO USE THIS STUFF.

HOW DO YOU KNOW?

BECAUSE, THIS IS THE CHRISTMAS WRAP YOU TOLD ME NOT TO THROW OUT **LAST** YEAR!!

SORRY I COULDN'T SEE YOU YESTERDAY.

THAT'S OK. I HAD TO SPEND TIME WITH MY FAMILY, TOO.

THANKS FOR THE LOCKET. I'VE NEVER OWNED ONE. —IT'S BEAUTIFUL.

YOU'RE WEARING THE SWEATER I GAVE YOU! DO YOU LIKE IT?

YES— BUT THE CARD THAT CAME WITH IT WAS EVEN BETTER.

YOU SIGNED IT: ♡ DEANNA!

WELL—A REAL VISIT AT LAST! CAN YOU STAY FOR DINNER, MICHAEL?

SURE, THAT WOULD BE NICE!

WE LIKE TO GET TO KNOW THE BOYS DEANNA GOES OUT WITH.

MR. SOBINSKI!

YES, IT'S ABOUT TIME WE HAD A CHANCE TO ACTUALLY TALK TO YOU!

I HAD THE "APPROVAL DINNER" AT YOUR PLACE... NOW, YOU GET TO HAVE THE "APPROVAL DINNER" AT MINE!

MICHAEL, WOULD YOU LIKE SOME TURKEY?

HERE— HAVE SOME SPUDS!

PASS HIM THE CORN, EVA!

GRAVY, HON?

TRY THE OAT BREAD. I MADE IT THIS MORNING.

NOW... TELL US ALL ABOUT YOURSELF.

HOW ARE YOUR DAD AND MICHAEL GETTING ALONG?

I'M NOT SURE...

DAD'S TELLING HIS "WHEN MY FATHER GOT OFF THE BOAT" STORY...

NOW, HE'S ONTO THE OL' "YOU YOUNG PEOPLE DON'T KNOW HOW GOOD YOU HAVE IT"

OK...WE'RE DOWN TO HIS JOKE ABOUT THE TWO GUYS FROM WARSAW

IS MICHAEL LAUGHING?

YESSS!

I THINK IT'S KIND OF WEIRD.... HOW PARENTS SAY THEY WANT TO KNOW THEIR KIDS' FRIENDS AND THEN **THEY** DO ALL THE TALKING!

MY PARENTS LIKE YOU, MICHAEL!

GOOD—THAT'S A RELIEF!!

NOW, WE'RE GOING OVER TO GORD AN' TRACEY'S. — I KNOW YOU'RE GOING TO GET ALONG WITH THEM!

WOW. HERE WE ARE, SEEKING THE APPROVAL OF EVERYONE, AND WHAT IF, NEXT YEAR, OUR RELATIONSHIP IS.......HISTORY?

I DON'T KNOW— I GUESS I'D HAVE TO START LIVING IN THE PAST!

SO, EVERYONE'S BACK IN SCHOOL NOW. THE HOUSE FEELS SO EMPTY.

LAWRENCE WENT TO PARIS THIS YEAR. IT WAS VERY STRANGE, NOT HAVING HIM HOME!

YES. WHEN THERE'S NO KIDS, I GUESS IT'S HARD TO GET EXCITED ABOUT CHRISTMAS.

OH, NOT REALLY...

WE BUY A LOT FOR THE DOG.

WAIT, CONNIE. I HAVE TO UNZIP MY JACKET. — I'M HAVING ANOTHER HOT FLASH.

YOU KNOW, THERE'S SOMETHING YOU CAN DO ABOUT THAT, EL.

ESTROGEN?

NO, I BELIEVE IN NATURAL WAYS TO RELIEVE DISCOMFORT.

SO DO I.

AAAAUGH!

IF YOU'RE SUFFERING FROM MENOPAUSE SYMPTOMS, YOU SHOULD TRY SOME HERBAL REMEDIES!

LOOK, EL! HERE'S A BRAND NEW BOTTLE OF EVENING PRIMROSE OIL CAPSULES.

WHAT'S THE MATTER, CONNIE — HAVING A HOT FLASH?

NO — I JUST PAID $13 FOR A LONG WAD OF COTTON!!!

RATTLE RATTLE

36

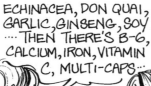

WHAK!

WHAP!

WHAK!

WHAP WHAK

WAP! SMAK

AHHH—THEY SAY THERE'S NOTHING LIKE YOUNG LOVE!

...BUT OLD LOVE IS BETTER.

Lynn

38

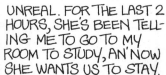

IS YOUR MOM OK, LIZ? SHE LOOKS TIRED.

I KNOW.

MY GRANDMA ISN'T WELL. MOM WANTED US ALL TO GO AND SEE HER AT CHRISTMAS... BUT GRANDMA SAID "NO."

SHE SAID SHE WAS FINE, AND SHE DIDN'T WANT US TO WORRY ABOUT HER...

SO, MOM'S BEEN WORRIED ABOUT HER EVER SINCE!

THANKS FOR COMING OVER, ANTHONY.

HEY- NO PROBLEM!

WAIT A MINUTE!

I WANT TO WALK OUT TO YOUR CAR WITH YOU.

HOW COME?

THIS IS THE ONE PLACE WHERE WE CAN'T BE SEEN!

41

I MADE ARRANGEMENTS TO FLY TO VANCOUVER NEXT WEEK, CONNIE. MY MOM AND DAD NEED SOME HELP RIGHT NOW.

I WAS SORRY TO BE LAID OFF AT WORK—BUT IT COULDN'T HAVE HAPPENED AT A BETTER TIME.

IT'S ALMOST AS IF SOMEBODY WORKED IT OUT THIS WAY! MAYBE YOU HAVE A GUARDIAN ANGEL!

I KNOW YOUR PARENTS DO!

WHY CAN'T I COME WITH YOU THIS TIME? BECAUSE YOU HAVE TO GO TO SCHOOL.

BUT I WANNA SEE GRANDMA MARIAN. I KNOW YOU DO, APRIL.

WHY DON'T YOU MAKE A SPECIAL CARD FOR ME TO TAKE TO HER. TELL HER HOW MUCH YOU LOVE HER.

... DO WE HAVE PAPER **BIG** ENOUGH?

LOOSE CHANGE, 3 RECEIPTS, GOLD PIN, TOOTHBRUSH....

EARRING, NAIL FILE, BUSINESS CARD, JELLY BEAN...

DID YOU CLEAN OUT THE SOFA?

I CLEANED OUT OUR SUITCASE.

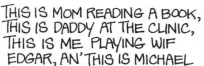

WHAT ARE YOU MAKING?
A BIG CARD FOR GRANDMA MARIAN.

THIS IS MOM READING A BOOK, THIS IS DADDY AT THE CLINIC, THIS IS ME PLAYING WIF EDGAR, AN' THIS IS MICHAEL DRIVING THE CAR.

SO WHERE'S ME?
THIS IS YOU, ... EATING.

I WANTED TO SHOW EVERYBODY DOING SOMETHING THEY REALLY LIKED!

ARE THOSE PEANUT BUTTER COOKIES, LIZ?
UH-HUH. THEY'RE GRANDPA'S FAVORITE.

CAN I HAVE ONE?
LATER, OK? WHEN I'VE FILLED UP THIS TIN, WE CAN HAVE WHAT'S LEFT.

ARE YOU GONNA FILL THE TIN NOW?
NO - WE HAVE TO WAIT UNTIL THE COOKIES ARE COOL, FIRST.

I WONDER WHY ELIZABETH DIDN'T THINK OF THIS!

APRIL, WHERE ARE ALL THE COOKIES I BAKED?
COOLING OFF!

I PUT THEM ALL OUTSIDE, ON THE PORCH.
WHICH PORCH?

CLICK!

WELL... AT LEAST WE KNOW THEY WERE GOOD!

SEE, JOHN?—HE'S DOING IT AGAIN!

HE DIGS UP ALL THE STUFF ON THE BOTTOM OF HIS CAGE AND THROWS IT EVERYWHERE!

I THINK HE'S JUST MAKING A NEST OR SOMETHING.

A LOT OF ANIMALS DO THAT BEFORE THEY LIE DOWN.

I KNOW... BUT HE'S NEVER REALLY BEEN AROUND OTHER RABBITS.

SO IT'S A PURELY NATURAL INSTINCT!

I THINK SO.

ON THE OTHER HAND... IT COULD BE "LEARNED BEHAVIOR."

DAD, MOM'S DOCTOR THINKS SHE SHOULD BE IN THE HOSPITAL. HE WANTS YOU TO GET SOME REST.

TOMORROW MORNING, THE AMBULANCE IS GOING TO COME AND TRANSFER HER. — DO YOU HEAR ME, DAD?

YES, DEAR.

IT'S THE BEST THING FOR YOU BOTH.

OK... WHATEVER YOU SAY, WE'LL DO.

WHAT'S FUNNY?

YOU USED TO TAKE ORDERS FROM **ME**!

WE'RE READY TO LIFT YOU UP NOW, MRS. RICHARDS. READY?

GO!

MY, YOU TWO BOYS ARE STRONG — AND HANDSOME, TOO!

MOM!

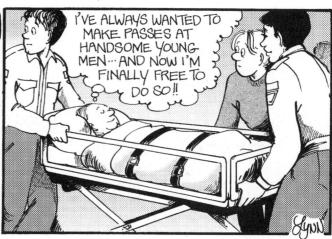

I'VE ALWAYS WANTED TO MAKE PASSES AT HANDSOME YOUNG MEN... AND NOW I'M FINALLY FREE TO DO SO!!

ARE YOU COMING TO THE HOSPITAL, DAD? I THINK MOM WOULD LIKE IT IF WE STAYED WITH HER AWHILE.

YES. I'LL BE THERE IN A MINUTE. I JUST WANT TO MAKE UP THE BED.

IT'S STILL WARM WHERE SHE WAS LYING.

...IT'S STILL WARM.

SCRAPE
SCRAPE

SLURRK...

Y'KNOW, MIKE.... MAYBE WE OUGHTA DO THE DISHES.

HERE'S THE ARTICLE THEY DID ON THE PHOTOS I HAD IN THE GALLERY.

"PORTRAIT" MAGAZINE! WEED, THIS IS GREAT!!

YEAH! — THEY QUOTED FROM THE STORIES YOU WROTE, TOO.

WE'RE TURNING OUT TO BE A GOOD TEAM — YOUR PICTURES AND MY TEXT! THIS COULD LEAD TO SOMETHING!

...LET'S HOPE IT'S CASH.

WOULDN'T IT BE COOL IF WE DID END UP WORKING TOGETHER?

TO TELL YOU THE TRUTH, WEED.... I DON'T REALLY KNOW WHERE I'M GOING.

I LIKE JOURNALISM, BUT I'M NOT AGGRESSIVE ENOUGH TO BE GOOD AT IT — AND I'D PROBABLY **STARVE** AS A NOVELIST!

MIKE... SOME DAY, I'M GONNA SEE YOU EAT THOSE WORDS!

THE WINE & DINER

THANKS FOR TAKING ME OUT FOR DINNER!

NO PROBLEM, LIZ!

ANTHONY... DO YOU THINK VALENTINE'S DAY WAS MADE FOR LOVERS OR FOR THE SAKE OF CRASS COMMERCIALISM?

CRASS COMMERCIALISM.

WHY?

'CAUSE, IF IT WAS FOR LOVERS... THEY'D HAVE MADE IT IN JULY!

53

55

DADDY, WHEN'S MOM COMING HOME?

I DON'T KNOW, APRIL. IT ALL DEPENDS ON HOW YOUR GRANDMA IS.

BESIDES, WE'RE MANAGING QUITE WELL ON OUR OWN.

WE'RE KEEPING THE HOUSE TIDY, I'M DOING THE LAUNDRY AND ELIZABETH'S LEARNING HOW TO COOK!

I KNOW.

THAT'S WHY I WANNA KNOW WHEN MOM'S COMING HOME.

APRIL, DON'T KICK OFF YOUR BOOTS WHEN YOU COME IN. STAND THEM ON THE MAT BY THE DOOR!

STOP TELLING ME WHAT TO DO. YOU'RE NOT MY MOM.

WELL, I'M IN CHARGE WHILE SHE'S AWAY, SO MOVE THOSE BOOTS!

NO!

FINE. THEN I'M GONNA TELL DAD WHEN HE COMES HOME.

SO? I'LL TELL HIM YOU YELLED AT ME!

AND TO THINK I ONCE SCOFFED AT PEOPLE WHO PREFER PETS TO CHILDREN.

IT'S WEIRD NOT HAVING MOM HOME, DAWN. APRIL'S A PAIN IN THE NECK—AN' I'VE GOTTA DO ALL THE COOKING!

I IRONED ALL THE CLOTHES LAST NIGHT—AN' I SHOULD HAVE BEEN STUDYING!!

I HATE ALL THIS RESPONSIBILITY. I'M NOT READY TO BE A PARENT YET! I'M STILL A KID! I WANNA LIVE LIKE A KID!

—I JUST WANT TO BE TREATED LIKE AN ADULT! ···· IS THAT SO DIFFICULT TO UNDERSTAND?

YES, JOHN. MOM IS STILL WITH US. WE'RE ALL TAKING SHIFTS AT THE HOSPITAL.

MY BROTHER IS WITH HER NOW.

STRANGE. HERE I AM, WATCHING MY MOTHER SLEEP. SHE LOOKS SO SMALL, WITH HER HAIR SPREAD OVER THE PILLOW. - AND I'M WONDERING....

HOW MANY TIMES DID YOU SIT LIKE THIS, AND WATCH OVER ME?

WOULD YOU LIKE ME TO TAKE OVER FOR A WHILE, PHIL?

SURE, SIS.

COME ON, DAD. LET'S GET A COFFEE.

HELLO, DEAR. EVERY TIME I OPEN MY EYES, I SEE A NEW FACE!

... AND I KEEP EXPECTING IT TO BE SAINT PETER.

MOM, I'D LIKE TO ASK YOU FOR A FAVOR.

YES, DEAR. ANYTHING.

IF IT'S POSSIBLE, WILL YOU WATCH OVER THE CHILDREN FOR ME? WHEN YOU GET TO...

HEAVEN? OF COURSE I WILL.

I PROMISE.

ONE THING ABOUT MY MOTHER IS... SHE ALWAYS KEEPS HER PROMISES.

I'M ACTUALLY STARTING TO ENJOY THE CUISINE NOW, SIS.

EVEN THE COFFEE'S OK.

EXCUSE ME, COULD YOU TELL ME WHERE THE X-RAY DEPARTMENT IS?

SURE!

RADIOLOGY

GO STRAIGHT TO THE MAIN ATRIUM, THEN RIGHT, PAST THE NEWS STAND, AND TAKE THE YELLOW ELEVATOR DOWN TO THE FIRST FLOOR.

YOU KNOW YOU'VE SPENT TOO MUCH TIME IN A HOSPITAL WHEN THE FOOD TASTES GOOD, YOU CAN GIVE DIRECTIONS, AND PEOPLE THINK YOU WORK HERE.

DAD, IT'S 4:00 A.M.—HOW LONG HAVE YOU BEEN SITTING THERE?

MOST OF THE NIGHT, I GUESS.

CAN I JOIN YOU?

I'D LIKE THAT.

I HAVEN'T WATCHED THE SUNRISE FOR A LONG TIME..

IT'S A GOOD THING TO DO ONCE IN A WHILE.

....MAKES YOU REALIZE THAT THE WORLD DOESN'T REVOLVE AROUND US.

RINGG!!

YES. WHEN? I SEE. WE'LL BE RIGHT THERE. THANK YOU.

MOM'S GONE, DAD. SHE WENT PEACEFULLY IN HER SLEEP.

GRANDMA MARIAN'S STILL IN VANCOUVER, APRIL—WHY?

I DON'T KNOW.. SHE JUST FEELS CLOSER, THAT'S ALL.

WE TOOK DAD TO SEE HER, JOHN. SHE LOOKED LIKE SHE WAS SLEEPING.

DAD HELD HER HAND. THE NURSE ASKED IF SHE SHOULD TAKE OFF MOM'S WEDDING BAND, BUT HE SAID "NO."

HE SAID THEY WERE POOR WHEN HE BOUGHT IT — BUT HE TOLD MOM SHE COULD HAVE ANY RING IN THE STORE.

IT WAS 1946. SHE CHOSE THE CHEAPEST ONE. IT COST TEN DOLLARS...

BUT WHEN HE PUT IT ON HER FINGER — IT WAS PRICELESS.

EVEN WHEN TIMES GOT BETTER, SHE NEVER WANTED ANOTHER RING.

THE TEN-DOLLAR WEDDING BAND WAS GOOD ENOUGH FOR HER.

IN 50 YEARS, MOM HAD NEVER TAKEN IT OFF HER FINGER.

AND DAD SAID SHE WASN'T GOING TO TAKE IT OFF NOW.

WITH DIFFICULTY, WE SAID GOOD-BYE.

OUTSIDE, IT WAS RAINING - BUT DAD WANTED TO WALK ALONG THE SEA WALL...THE WAY HE AND MOM USED TO DO.

WE WONDERED HOW HE'D LIVE WITHOUT HER — HOW WE ALL WOULD.

BUT YOU'RE NEVER TOO OLD TO LEARN FROM YOUR FATHER.

HE LEFT US AT THE LIGHTHOUSE... AND WALKED ALONE.

Art supplies

Wrapping Paper

HOW ABOUT CLEANING UP, NOW.

OK, DAD-WE'RE JUST WAITING FOR THE NEWS TO COME ON.

WELL, I'M GLAD TO SEE THAT MY KIDS ARE FINALLY INTERESTED IN WHAT'S GOING ON IN THE WORLD!

HELLO, THIS IS PETER MANSBRIDGE, WITH THE C B C EVENING NEWS....

63

HI, TRACEY! THOUGHT I'D FILL UP ON THE WAY HOME.

SURE! GORDON'S INSIDE.

IT'S GOING GOOD THIS MONTH, DOC! THE TWO GUYS I HIRED ARE PAYING FOR THEMSELVES, AND IT SEEMS LIKE WE'RE GETTING NEW CUSTOMERS EVERY DAY.

CHECK IT OUT—WE'RE CONSISTENTLY IN THE BLACK! GREAT NEWS.

—AND IT LOOKS AS THOUGH YOUR SON IS, TOO!

WE'RE RUNNING OUT OF SPACE IN THE SHOP, DOC. CAN'T MANAGE ALL THE JOBS WE HAVE.

AT SOME POINT, WE'RE GONNA HAVE TO BUILD ANOTHER BAY!

I WAS THINKING ABOUT THAT.

IF YOU PUT ON ANOTHER BAY, GORD— YOU COULD ADD ON TO YOUR APARTMENT!

WHAT MAKES YOU THINK WE NEED THE SPACE?!

WE'D LIKE TO ADD ON TO THIS PLACE, DOC— BUT WE WANT TO PAY YOU BACK FIRST.

WHAT FOR? WE'RE HAPPY WITH OUR INVESTMENT. BESIDES, SOME DAY WHEN YOU'RE A BIG SUCCESS, WE CAN SAY WE WERE PART OF IT!

THANKS FOR ALL OF YOUR HELP AND ENCOURAGEMENT, DR. P.

ENCOURAGEMENT IS THE EASY PART, TRACEY.

IT'S YOU WHO ARE DOING ALL THE WORK!

WHO ARE YOU E-MAIL-ING?

MY FRIEND GORDON.

MY DAD TOLD HIM THAT MY GRANDMOTHER PASSED AWAY. HE JUST WROTE TO SAY HE WAS SORRY.

I SHOULD WRITE TO MY GRANDFATHER, BUT I DON'T KNOW WHAT TO SAY.

SAY ANYTHING, MICHAEL.

THIS IS ONE TIME WHEN A WORD IS WORTH A THOUSAND PICTURES!

THE FLOWERS KEEP COMING, ELLY. SO MANY PEOPLE LOVED YOUR MOTHER.

I'M PUTTING THE CARDS AND LETTERS INTO AN ALBUM, SO I CAN READ THEM AGAIN.

DAD-I HAVE TO GO HOME SOON.

I KNOW. I'VE BEEN TRYING NOT TO THINK ABOUT IT.

AND... I WANT YOU TO COME WITH ME.

GRAMPA'S COMING HOME WITH MOM?—COOL!

YAH!

IT'S NOT A PERMANENT THING, NECESSARILY. WE'RE GOING TO TRY IT AND SEE HOW IT WORKS OUT.

HEY, DON'T WORRY, DAD -IT'LL WORK OUT GREAT!

I'M GLAD YOU THINK SO, LIZ...

WE'D LIKE HIM TO HAVE YOUR ROOM!

YOU WANT GRAMPA TO HAVE MY ROOM? ..FOR HOW LONG, DAD?

AS LONG AS HE LIKES, HONEY.— YOU'LL BE MOVING TO MICHAEL'S ROOM.

BUT I DON'T REALLY WANT MICHAEL'S ROOM.

WELL, YOU CAN'T HAVE MINE!

THIS ISN'T A CASE OF WHAT ANYONE WANTS... IT'S WHAT HAS TO HAPPEN.

HE NEEDS HIS OWN SPACE, AND HIS OWN BATHROOM—AND THERE'S ONLY ONE BEDROOM IN THE HOUSE THAT WILL GIVE HIM THAT.

YOURS!!

ARE YOU SURE THAT JOHN AND THE KIDS DON'T MIND IF I STAY AWHILE?

OF COURSE NOT, DAD. THEY'RE LOOKING FORWARD TO IT! THERE'S GOING TO BE A ROOM ALL READY FOR YOU WHEN WE GET THERE.

THE QUESTION IS.. HOW DO YOU FEEL ABOUT COMING TO STAY WITH US?

... LIKE I'M RUNNING AWAY FROM HOME.

WHEN MOM COMES HOME WITH GRANDPA, LET'S SMILE, OK? HE SHOULDN'T SEE US LOOKING SAD.

BUT, I AM SAD.

WHY DO SAD THINGS HAVE TO HAPPEN, ELIZABETH? WHY CAN'T WE JUST BE HAPPY ALL THE TIME?

I DON'T KNOW, APRIL.

IT'S KIND OF HARD TO EXPLAIN. IT SEEMS YOU CAN'T HAVE ONE THING WITHOUT THE OTHER. HAPPY AND SAD ARE LIKE... WELL, SUNSHINE AND SHADOW.

AND, GRANDMA WAS SUNSHINE.

THERE'S A PARCEL ON THE TABLE FOR YOU, MIKE.

YEAH?

OH, MAN, THIS IS SO COOL. MY MOM IS THE BEST!

WHAT'D SHE SEND?

TWO PAIRS OF SOCKS, A T-SHIRT AN' SOME UNDERWEAR.

LUCKY.

YEAH. NOW I DON'T HAVE TO DO LAUNDRY FOR ANOTHER TWO WEEKS!

WEED? MAYBE WE SHOULD GO OUT TO EAT.

YOU THINK?

CLUNK, CLUNK

YEAH. THIS PLACE CAN GET TO YOU SOMETIMES.

TRUE.

SCRAPE

SO, LET'S GO GRAB A SUB OR SOME WINGS, AN' GET OUTTA THE KITCHEN.

BONE IDEA.

... THEN WE WON'T HAFTA MESS IT UP.

SO, THEY'VE GOT ME AT THIS MAGAZINE, PROOF-READING, RIGHT?

BUT THE COPY'S BEEN BY TWO EDITORS ALREADY — AN' I'M UP AGAINST "SPELL-CHECK" — SO.... SPELL "REDUNDANT"!

LIKE, WHAT'S THE POINT?

THE POINT IS — PLACEMENT GIVES YOU A FOOT IN THE DOOR!

YOU'RE TELLING ME. WANNA CHECK OUT THE SWELLING?

DEFINITE SIGNS OF INJURY.

I'M CUTTING THE NEWS AT CPOP RADIO. THEY GIVE IT 05 MINUTES EVERY HOUR ON THE HALF, AN' IT'S LIKE, FAST!

WE'RE INTO THIS FOR THE NUMBERS — ANYONE WHO DUMPS THE COMPETITION AN' SURFS THE AIR — WE GOTTA GRAB 'EM AN' HOLD THEIR ATTENTION!

SO, WE'RE DOING, LIKE THE HOT HEADLINES, FAST-FORWARD INTO SPORTS, AN' **BAM!** LEAD INTO THE NEXT HIT BEFORE COMMERCIAL!

MIND YOU, IF THERE WERE A REAL DISASTER, LIKE A WAR OR SOMETHING, WE'D SWITCH TO S & S MODE… "SLOW AN' SINCERE."

YOU STILL DOGGING SOME REPORTER AT THE STAR, MIKE?

NOT RIGHT NOW, MAL.

I GOT A PROJECT WITH WEED APPROVED. — I'M DOING TRUE, SHORT STORIES TO GO WITH HIS PHOTOGRAPHS.

SO FAR, WE'VE HAD 3 GALLERY SHOWS…

WHAT ARE YOU GONNA DO-COFFEE TABLE BOOKS?

HEY, COOL IDEA! - JUST MAKE 'EM BIG ENOUGH TO SCREW LEGS ON, IF THEY DON'T SELL!

I'M NOT GONNA BE A JOURNALIST, WEED. NOT LIKE SOME OF THE GUYS WE KNOW.

YOU'RE NOT GONNA BE A REPORTER, YOU MEAN.

I JUST WANT TO WRITE WHAT I FEEL, WHAT I KNOW. — IT'S NOT STUFF YOU CAN LEARN…IT JUST IS!!

SO…YOU WANT TO BE A STARVING ARTIST!

IF I HAVE TO STARVE TO DO WHAT I WANT TO DO-THEN I'LL STARVE!

THAT REMINDS ME… WE'RE OUTTA FOOD!

IS THAT AN E-MAIL FROM MICHAEL?—WHAT DOES IT SAY?!!

OH... PERSONAL THINGS JUST...STUFF.

HOW COME YOU NEVER TELL ME ANYTHING?

'CAUSE YOU'RE A BLABBERMOUTH. YOU ALWAYS TELL MOM.

I DO NOT!

YOU DO SO!

MOMMM!

MOM

NOT NOW, HONEY—I'M ON THE PHONE.

WHAT'S THE MATTER, APRIL?

ELIZABETH'S BUGGING ME, GRAMPA—SHE STUCK HER TONGUE OUT AT ME.

SHE DID?—WELL, WE'LL FIX THAT.

SNUFFL

GRAMPA..WHY DOES IT TAKE SO LONG TO BE BIG?

WELL, APRIL, I THINK TIME GOES MORE SLOWLY FOR PEOPLE YOUR AGE.

REALLY?

UH-HUH. IT DOESN'T SPEED UP UNTIL YOU'RE ABOUT 20 — AND BY THE TIME YOU'RE 40, THE YEARS GO FLYING BY!!

AND WHEN YOU'RE OLD? WELL....IT SORT OF SLOWS DOWN AGAIN.

HOW COME?

...SO WE CAN SEE THE WORLD THROUGH THE EYES OF OUR GRAND-CHILDREN.

WELL, WHERE HAVE YOU TWO BEEN?

AT THE PARK—AN' GUESS WHAT, THEY FIXED THE MERRY-GO-ROUND!

I HELD ON TIGHT, AN' GRAMPA PUSHED ME 'ROUND AN' ROUND AN' ROUND!

YOU DON'T LOOK TOO MERRY, DAD—DID YOU RUN OUT OF GAS?

OH, NO—I'VE GOT PLENTY OF GAS.

··· I JUST DON'T HAVE MUCH ENERGY.

YOUR DAD'S BEEN LIVING WITH YOU FOR A COUPLE OF WEEKS, NOW, EL—HOW'S IT WORKING OUT?

OK, I THINK. HE HAS HIS SAD TIMES, BUT HE'S COPING WELL··· AND THE KIDS HAVE BRIGHTENED HIS SPIRITS.

THEY GIVE HIM A NEW PERSPECTIVE?

···THEY GIVE HIM A NEW AUDIENCE.

DURING THE WAR···

DID YOU SEE LOTS OF FIGHTING DURING THE WAR, GRAMPA?

SOME··· FROM THE AIR, MOSTLY.

WE FLEW BOMBERS FROM ENGLAND OVER THE CHANNEL. THE TOUGHEST RAIDS WERE AT NIGHT.

ONE TIME, SUDSY RYAN AND I SNUCK UP BEHIND A RE-CONNAISSANCE PLANE — JUST BARELY VISIBLE BY THE LIGHT OF THE MOON···

MOM! DID YOU HEAR GRAMPA'S STORY ABOUT THE ENEMY PILOT AN' THE PARA-CHUTE?

YES, APRIL!

ALL 4 VERSIONS AND OVER 2,000 TIMES.

HAHAHAHAHA HAHAHAHA HA!!!

IT'S NICE TO SEE YOU TWO ENJOYING YOUR GRANDPA'S STORIES.

YEAH—HE'S GOT SOME GREAT ONES!

IF THERE'S ONE THING HE REMEMBERS IN DETAIL, IT'S THE WAR!

OH, HE WASN'T TELLING US ABOUT THE WAR, MOM...

...HE WAS TELLING US ABOUT YOU!

GRANDPA WANTED A SINGALONG... SO, I GUESS THIS IS IT.

HOW'S IT GOING, EL?

OH... HABBING DAD AROUMB TAKES A BIK OB GEDDING USED TO.

HE HAS HIS GOOD DAYS AND BAD... AND HE STILL DOES ALL THE THINGS THAT USED TO DRIVE ME CRAZY.

GRRBBL

STILL, YOU HAVE TO BE ABLE TO LIVE WITH PEOPLE, AND ACCEPT THEM FOR WHO THEY ARE...

WHONK!

AFTER ALL— WE EACH HAVE OUR ECCENTRICITIES.

FLAP FLAP

EVERY DAY I TRY TO LOOK HAPPY. I TRY TO BE FUNNY ..... I TRY TO COPE. BUT I MISS YOU SO MUCH, MARIAN!!

I FEEL LIKE A KID AGAIN; LOST IN A BIG, STRANGE BED...AFRAID TO BE ALONE...

WELL, HELLO, EDGAR. WHAT ARE YOU DOING HERE?

YOU WANT UP? ...YOU'RE NOT SUPPOSED TO BE ON THE BED.

FINE! — IF YOU INSIST.

I WAS JUST ABOUT TO SPEND ANOTHER MISERABLE NIGHT FEELING SORRY FOR MYSELF.

... HOW DID YOU KNOW?

SO, EDGAR-WHAT'S NEXT? WHAT AM I GOING TO DO WITH MY LIFE?

DO I GO HOME AND LIVE IN THE LITTLE HOUSE IN BRITISH COLUMBIA, OR DO I MOVE IN HERE WITH MY DAUGHTER?

BUT I GUESS I DON'T HAVE TO MAKE THAT DECISION NOW, DO I. I HAVE ENOUGH TO DEAL WITH AS IT IS.

THERE'S NOTHING LIKE TALKING THINGS OVER WITH A FRIEND.

MAN, STUDENT PARKING IS GETTING CRAZY!

YEAH, YOU GOTTA BE HERE BY 8 IF YOU WANT A GOOD SPOT!

THERE! OVER BY THE DOOR.

THAT'S A LOADING AREA, DAWN.

AN' I WON'T PARK THERE ... THAT'S FOR THE BOTTOM FEEDERS.

HOW CAN YOU TELL?

THEY MARK THEIR TERRITORY.

MAN, I DIDN'T KNOW THAT THE BOTTOM FEEDERS HAD A DESIGNATED PARKING AREA!

YEAH...

THOSE GUYS USUALLY PARK TOGETHER, THE JOCKS PARK BY THE GYM, AN' THE COOL TYPES PARK OVER HERE, BY THE CAFETERIA.

SHOOT! THERE ISN'T EVEN A SPACE ON NERD ROW!!

THIS IS SO AMAZING!

IT'S JUST A MICROCOSM OF SOCIETY, DAWN.... YOU'VE GOT TO FIND YOUR SPOT IN THE PARKING LOT OF LIFE.

YOU CAN'T PARK HERE, LIZ. IT'S FOR TEACHERS ONLY.

I KNOW.

WHAT IF YOUR CAR GETS TOWED AWAY?

IT WON'T.

NOBODY CAN TELL THE DIFFERENCE BETWEEN MY CAR AN' A TEACHER'S CAR...

—IT'S AN OLD ONE.

81

I WONDER WHY NATURE DEVELOPED THE TWO SEXES.

SO WE COULD PROCREATE!

I THINK IT WOULD BE BETTER IF WE JUST DIVIDED LIKE MICROBES.

HOW, LIZ? TOP-TO-BOTTOM, DOWN THE CENTER... OR AT THE WAIST?

TOP-TO-BOTTOM, OF COURSE! IF WE DIVIDED AT THE WAIST, HALF OF US WOULD BE BRAINS, AN' THE OTHER HALF WOULD BE BUTTS!!

HOWEVER, ONE WONDERS SOMETIMES IF THAT HASN'T ALREADY HAPPENED!!

HELLOOoo

WHAT ARE YOU GONNA WEAR TO GRADUATION, LIZ?

OH, SOMETHING OF MY MOM'S.

MAN!...I'D NEVER WEAR ONE OF MY MOM'S DRESSES.

NEITHER WOULD I.

WHY NOT?

DON'T THEY HAVE ANYTHING NICE?

SURE THEY DO!

WE'RE JUST NOT READY TO ADMIT IT!!

RINSE
RINSE
RINSE

GRAPE
DRINK
CRYSTALS

HI, DAD! WHERE HAVE YOU BEEN?

OH, I WENT DOWN TO THE SENIORS' CENTER TO LOOK AROUND.

I WANTED TO SEE IF I'D FIT IN — BUT I DON'T THINK SO....

....TOO MANY OLD PEOPLE.

YOU WERE DOWN AT THE SENIORS' CENTER A LONG TIME, DAD.... FOR A PLACE YOU DON'T BELONG!

I KNOW. I ONLY INTENDED TO GET SOME INFORMATION.

BUT THEN AN EMERGENCY HAPPENED, AND THEY ASKED FOR MY ASSISTANCE.

... ONE OF THE GENTS THERE NEEDED A GAME OF CRIBBAGE.

SO, YOU FOUND A CRIBBAGE PARTNER!

I'M TRYING, EL.

EVERY DAY, I TRY TO PICK UP THE PIECES AND LOOK AHEAD, BUT IT'S SO HARD.

I KNOW. I MISS MOM, TOO.

BEING WITHOUT HER IS LIKE NO OTHER PAIN I CAN IMAGINE.

WHAT'S THIS?

NOTHING ... I JUST NEEDED TO GIVE YOU A HUG.

WHAT ARE YOU LOOKING AT?

YOU DON'T WANT TO BE AROUND A MISERABLE OLD MAN — GO FIND SOMETHING ELSE TO DO.

OK, SUIT YOURSELF.

BUT DON'T BE SURPRISED IF I IGNORE YOU.

HOW'S YOUR DAD, EL?

HE'S MANAGING, CONNIE.

HE WENT THROUGH OUR FAMILY PHOTOGRAPHS LAST WEEK. THEY BROUGHT BACK A LOT OF MEMORIES.

I CAN SEE WHY IT TOOK HIM SO LONG TO GO THROUGH YOUR PHOTOS. — LOOK AT ALL THE ALBUMS!

I KNOW.

THEY WERE IN BOXES WHEN HE STARTED!

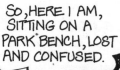

SO, HERE I AM, SITTING ON A PARK BENCH, LOST AND CONFUSED.

WHAT'S NEXT, EDGAR? HOW DOES A 75-YEAR OLD MAN BEGIN HIS LIFE ALL OVER AGAIN?

WHAT AM I SUPPOSED TO DO... SURVIVE EACH DAY AS IT COMES AND MAKE THE BEST OF IT?

I GUESS THAT'S ALL I **CAN** DO, ISN'T IT.

ONE THING ABOUT YOU, ED..... YOU ALWAYS GIVE GOOD ADVICE.

THERE YOU ARE, EDGAR!

HE TOOK ME FOR A WALK IN THE PARK.

YOU LIKE HIM, DON'T YOU, GRAMPA.

UH-HUH. YOUR GRANDMA NEVER WANTED A DOG IN THE HOUSE.

SHE SAID THEY WERE NOISY, MESSY AND ALWAYS WANTED ATTENTION...

AND SHE ALREADY HAD ME.

WHATCHA DOING NOW, GRAMPA?

KEEPING MYSELF BUSY.

LAST WEEK, I PUT ALL THE PHOTOGRAPHS INTO ALBUMS. TODAY I WANT TO START ON THE SLIDES.

HOLY COW!

WHAT?

WELL ... SHE DID SAY THEY WERE ORGANIZED.

THIS IS WONDERFUL. SO MANY OF THESE PICTURES I'VE NEVER SEEN!

MICHAEL WHEN HE WAS 5, LIZ WHEN SHE WAS A BRAND NEW BABY, THE FIRST HOUSE YOUR MOM AND DAD BOUGHT...

HERE'S MIKE IN HIS PEE WEE HOCKEY UNIFORM, LIZ'S 3RD BIRTHDAY. NOW, I THINK THESE ARE IN SEQUENCE.-IS ANYTHING MISSING?

YES!!

ME!!

THERE AREN'T ANY PICTURES OF ME HERE, GRAMPA.

THAT'S 'CAUSE YOU WEREN'T BORN WHEN THEY WERE TAKEN, APRIL.

YOUR DAD TOOK COLOR SLIDES WHEN MICHAEL WAS LITTLE, AND AFTER LIZ WAS BORN, HE WENT BACK TO TAKING PRINTS.

THEY USED A POLAROID FOR A WHILE BECAUSE IT WAS SO FAST.... AND YOU CAME ALONG MUCH LATER.

THEY MUST HAVE BEEN WAITING FOR VIDEO.

I SHOWED APRIL HOW TO USE THE SLIDE PROJECTOR, ELLY. SHE'S HAVING A GREAT TIME.

I GUESS SHE'S SO USED TO TELEVISION THAT SEEING LARGE, STILL PHOTOGRAPHS IS A BIT OF A NOVELTY.

IT'S NICE TO SEE A NEW GENERATION APPRECIATE AN OLD TECHNOLOGY.

HEY, UGLY BROTHER! WE WATCHED A BUNCH OF OLD SLIDES LAST NIGHT. IT WAS COOL!

REMEMBER WHEN YOU AND GORDON BLEW UP PINK RUBBER GLOVES AND ACTED LIKE COWS? REMEMBER THE SOCK-SNIFFING CONTEST?

THERE WERE SO MANY GREAT PICTURES OF YOU DOING THE DUMBEST THINGS!!!

HOW MUCH TO KEEP THEM OFF THE INTERNET?

CLICK TICK!

IF YOU'RE SENDING A MESSAGE TO MICHAEL, LIZ—ASK HIM WHEN HE'S COMING HOME.

I DID.

AND?

HE'S NOT SURE. HE MIGHT STAY IN LONDON AND WORK ON A PROJECT WITH HIS ROOMMATE.

WHAT ABOUT HIS JOB AT MEGAFOOD?

I APPLIED FOR IT. HIS BOSS SAID HE'D TRY AN' GET ME ON DAY SHIFT.

WHY AM I ALWAYS THE LAST TO KNOW EVERYTHING?

YOU'RE NOT ON-LINE!

MICHAEL AN' I SEND MESSAGES BACK AN' FORTH ALL THE TIME, MOM—AND WE GO INTO THESE CHAT-ROOMS ... SEE?

YOU MEAN YOU JUST TALK TO WHOEVER HAPPENS TO BE THERE?

SURE!

WHAT DO YOU TALK ABOUT?

HOMEWORK, MOVIES, PERSONAL STUFF ... YOU JUST OPEN UP AN' SAY WHATEVER YOU WANNA SAY!

ISN'T IT DANGEROUS?

YEAH... MY WRISTS GET A LITTLE SORE SOMETIMES.

MICHAEL, ELIZABETH SAYS YOU'RE NOT COMING HOME THIS SUMMER.

UH-HUH... THERE'S STUFF I WANT TO DO HERE.

BESIDES, I FIGURED THAT WITH GRANDPA THERE, YOU DIDN'T NEED ANOTHER BODY IN THE HOUSE.

BUT...

HEY, I'LL BE AROUND. I'LL SEE YOU, MOM! DON'T FORGET, I'M 22—I DON'T **LIVE** THERE ANYMORE!

FOR YEARS, YOU TELL THEM TO "GROW UP"— AND THEN, ONE DAY .... THEY REALLY DO.

SO, MICHAEL'S NOT COMING HOME!—LAWRENCE HASN'T LIVED WITH US FOR 3 YEARS, ELLY.

I KNOW.

IT'S JUST HARD TO BELIEVE THAT OUR BOYS ARE ADULTS.

WAIT 'TIL HE STARTS ASKING YOU ABOUT AGING!

YOU KNOW, HEALTH QUESTIONS, HOW DO YOU FEEL ABOUT WHAT YOU'VE ACCOMPLISHED IN LIFE, LOSING YOUR LOOKS, THAT SORT OF THING.

HE THINKS YOU'RE GETTING OLD?

...HE THINKS HE IS!

CONNIE, I WAS LOOKING IN THE MIRROR THE OTHER DAY—AND I'M GETTING A DOUBLE CHIN.

WHAT DO YOU THINK?

WELL, IF YOU PUT YOUR HEAD DOWN LIKE THAT, OF COURSE YOU ARE !!!

TILT IT BACK LIKE THIS. GOOD. NOW, PUT YOUR JAW FORWARD A LITTLE AND....SMILE.

THERE. YOU SEE? —YOU LOOK PERFECTLY NORMAL.

I THINK IT'S FUNNY.

WHAT ARE YOU TALKING ABOUT, DAD?

YOU. WORRIED ABOUT LOOKING OLDER.

YOU'RE PERFECT, DEAR. YOU'RE YOUNG AND SWEET AND ABSOLUTELY BEAUTIFUL!

... YOU LOOK JUST LIKE YOUR MOTHER.

CLANK!
RATTLE
RATTLE
RATTLE
CLINK!

THESE ARE FROM ME .... AND FROM DADDY!

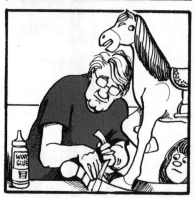

HOW LONG ARE YOU GOING TO STAY WITH US, GRAMPA?

PUT IT THIS WAY....AS LONG AS I'M NEEDED.

WHAT ARE YOU DOING, APRIL?

LOOKING FOR SOMETHING TO BREAK.

95

OH, YOU'RE AWRIGHT. IF SUMMAT WERE OUTTA PLACE, YOU WOULDN'T BE GETTING UP SO EASY.

I TOLD YOU TO STAY OFF THE ROOF! "YOU'LL FALL OFF AN' HURT Y'SELF!" DIDN'T I SAY THAT?

AND WHAT DO YOU BOYS DO? GO UP AN' LIE ON THE BLEEDIN' ROOF, FER PETE'S SAKE! —WELL, YOU DESERVE A BRUISING!

AN' HERE I AM, DISHING OUT SYMPATHY WHEN I SHOULD BE TELLING YOU OFF!!!

THANKS FOR PATCHING ME UP, MRS. DINGLE.

BETTER THAN LETTING YOU BLEED ALL OVER MY ROCK GARDEN.

WHAT ARE YOU STARING AT THEN?

IS THIS A PORTRAIT OF YOUR HUSBAND?

THAT'S HIM. BOBBY DINGLE. ONE OF A KIND, HE WAS! HE LOVED TO WORK, HE LOVED TO DRINK AND HE LOVED TO FIGHT. —AN' WHEN HE WASN'T WORKIN' OR DRINKIN' OR FIGHTING..

... HE LOVED ME.

HOW ARE YOU, MIKE?

OK. MRS. DINGLE CLEANED OUT A COUPLE OF CUTS FOR ME.

I NEVER THINK OF HER AS A "PARENT TYPE," BUT NOW AND THEN SHE REALLY ACTS LIKE MY MOTHER.

WHAT DID SHE GIVE YOU — ADVICE?

BETTER THAN THAT—

BUTTER TARTS!!

HI, GRAMPS! 'BYE, GRAMPS!

ELLY, WHAT'S GOING ON?

THIS HAPPENS EVERY YEAR ABOUT NOW, DAD — IT'S "SPRING FEVER"!

OH.

I THOUGHT MAYBE IT WAS THE "NUTS IN MAY."

PACKING ALREADY?

YEAH. I WANT TO CATCH THE EARLY BUS.

HOW LONG WILL YOU BE GONE?

A COUPLE OF WEEKS. WE'RE GOING TO MY GRANDMOTHER'S MEMORIAL SERVICE.

IT'S GOING TO BE A REAL FAMILY REUNION!

I WENT TO ONE OF THOSE ONCE - AN' DISCOVERED I'D INHERITED SOMETHING FROM MY GREAT-GRANDFATHER!

HIS MONEY?

HIS NOSE.

HERE, DEANNA. WOULD YOU LIFT THIS INTO THE TRUNK FOR ME?

SURE. WHAT'S WRONG?

NOTHING. I JUST HURT MY BACK A LITTLE.

HE FELL OFF THE BLINKIN' ROOF, MY DEAR - AN' IT'S A REAL GOOD JOB HE DIDN'T DO HISSELF IN!!

I'D HAVE HAD TO GO LOOKING FOR A NEW RENTER.

TAKE MY KEYS. YOU TWO GO TO THE BUS. DEANNA CAN BRING THE CAR BACK.

THANKS, WEED.

I'LL DRIVE. YOU TAKE IT EASY.

YOU KNOW, DEANNA ....IT FEELS LIKE I HAVE TWO FAMILIES, MY FRIENDS AND MY RELATIVES!

IT'S TOO BAD YOU CAN'T CHOOSE YOUR RELATIVES, TOO - ISN'T IT!

I DON'T KNOW..

I'D CHOOSE TO BE RELATED TO YOU, IF YOU CHOSE TO BE RELATED TO ME!

JO SAID YOU SPENT YOUR LAST DIME REPLACING MRS. D'S SCREEN DOOR... SO, HERE'S 20 BUCKS.

UH, THANKS, DEANNA.

HEY, I KNOW YOU'RE PRETENDING YOU DIDN'T HEAR ME WHEN I SAID I'D LIKE TO BE RELATED TO YOU.

I KNOW YOU'RE NOT READY TO MAKE A COMMITMENT, SO I'LL STOP DROPPING HINTS ABOUT IT.

GOOD.

THANKS FOR DRIVING ME TO THE BUS STATION.

ANY TIME.

I'LL GIVE YOU A RING WHEN I GET HOME.

TORONTO

EXCUSE ME, WHEN WILL THE BUS FROM LONDON BE HERE?

15 MINUTES, BAY 5.

THIS IS SO WEIRD. I CAN'T WAIT TO SEE MICHAEL. I NEVER THOUGHT I'D BE SO EXCITED ABOUT MEETING MY BROTHER!

IS THAT ELIZABETH? - SHE'S COME TO MEET ME! THIS IS SO WEIRD. I NEVER THOUGHT I'D BE SO EXCITED ABOUT SEEING MY SISTER!

HIYA, SISTWIRP.

HEY, UGLY BROTHER.

SO, GRANDMA'S MEMORIAL SERVICE IS TURNING INTO A MAJOR PRODUCTION.

YEAH. MOM'S BEEN ON THE PHONE ALL WEEK. SEEMS LIKE MOST OF THE FAMILY WILL BE THERE.

SOME OF OUR RELATIVES HAVE ONLY SEEN APRIL IN THOSE FAMILY PORTRAITS WE SEND AT CHRISTMAS!

I KNOW.

IT'LL BE NICE TO SHOW THEM THE REAL THING!

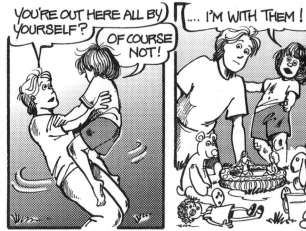

WHOA! WHAT ARE YOU ALL DRESSED UP FOR?

MY GRADUATION CEREMONY IS TONIGHT, REMEMBER? EVERYONE'S GOING TO MY GRAD, AN' THEN WE GO OUT WEST WITH GRANDPA.

YOU'RE STARING.

YEAH... I'VE NEVER SEEN YOU LOOK **GOOD** BEFORE!

TSK: SHE STILL DOESN'T KNOW HOW TO ACCEPT A COMPLIMENT.

OH MY, ELIZABETH! IS THAT REALLY YOU?

ISN'T IT NICE TO SEE YOUR SISTER ALL GROWN UP LIKE THIS, MICHAEL?

SO POISED, SO MATURE - SUCH A LOVELY YOUNG LADY.

-BRAPPTThhh

BRUSH COMB BRUSH BRUSH

AAAGHH! I WILL NOT GO TO MY GRAD LOOKING LIKE **THIS**!

NO MATTER WHAT I DO, I CAN'T GET MY HAIR TO GO RIGHT!

HERE. LET ME HELP YOU.

NOW. THAT'S PERFECT. YOU LOOK BEAUTIFUL.

THANKS, MOM.

AND, AS WE SAY FAREWELL TO FAMILIAR FACES AND FAMILIAR PLACES, THE GRADUATING CLASS OF 1998 ...

IT MAKES YOU OPTIMISTIC ABOUT THE FUTURE, DOESN'T IT, DAD?

WE'VE PRODUCED A WHOLE GENERATION OF YOUNG PEOPLE WHO ARE DETERMINED TO MAKE THIS WORLD A BETTER PLACE!

I KNOW...

SO DID WE.

OH, MAN—MY DAD'S OUT THERE WITH THE VIDEO CAMERA.

HE'S STANDING RIGHT OUT FRONT—AN' I BEGGED HIM **NOT** TO!!!

THIS IS SO TOTALLY EMBARRASSING!!!

YEAH. BUMMER.

REALLY.

CAN I GET A COPY?

ME TOO?

YO!

OVER HERE

SO, NOW IT'S OFF TO THE DANCE!

DON'T WAIT UP FOR ME, OK?

HAVE A GOOD TIME, HONEY.

:SNORT: WELL, THAT'S JUST FINE. NICE WAY TO START OFF AN ALL-NIGHT PARTY.

WHAT DID SHE SAY?

WE TRUST YOU.

WHEW! — I'M GLAD THAT'S OVER!

ME TOO.

...NOW, WE CAN **PARTY!**

GOOD THING WE BROUGHT A CHANGE OF CLOTHES!

YEAH. I COULDN'T WAIT TO GET OUT OF THAT DRESS!

SO, WE'RE GOING TO CLUB SODA, THEN TO GRAHAM'S FOR THE ALL-NIGHTER, AN' O'GRADYS ARE HAVING A PANCAKE BREAKFAST.

WHAT DO YOU THINK, ANTHONY — SHOULD WE TRY AN' PARTY FOR 24 HOURS STRAIGHT?

WHY NOT?

— WE GOTTA START PREPARING FOR UNIVERSITY!!

HI, HONEY. HOW WAS THE PARTY?

DID YOU STAY OUT ALL NIGHT, ELIZABETH?

YEAH. IT WAS COOL! WE WENT TO ABOUT 4 PLACES AN' HAD A PANCAKE BREAKFAST AT 5 A.M., THEN A BUNCH OF US WENT TO THE PARK!!

YOU MUST BE EXHAUSTED!

NAH. I JUST CAME HOME TO TAKE A SHOWER.

CRASHHHHHH

HEY, LOOKIT THIS! AN OLD-FASHIONED CANDY MACHINE!

COOL!

GOT ANY CHANGE, LIZ?

SURE.

CLAKKITY KLAK

GEE, I WISH I HAD A SMALL BAG OR SOMETHING.

GOT ONE!

HEY, THAT'S COOL! DO YOU ALWAYS WALK AROUND WITH A PLASTIC BAG IN YOUR POCKET?

NOPE....

JUST WHEN I WALK THE DOG.

EDDY! HOW'S MY BOY? WANNA GO FOR A **CAR** RIDE?

COME ON! CAR RIDE, EDGAR! **LET'S GO!**

DADDY, HE KNOWS YOU'RE TAKING HIM SOMEPLACE HE DOESN'T WANT TO GO. WHY DON'T YOU JUST BE HONEST AN' TELL HIM HE'S GOING TO THE KENNEL?

ANIMALS AND LITTLE KIDS. .... THEY'RE ALWAYS SMARTER THAN THEY LOOK.

TOO BAD YOU HAVE TO GO TO VANCOUVER FOR A FUNERAL, LIZ.

IT'S A MEMORIAL SERVICE, DAWN. I THINK IT'S DIFFERENT.

I'VE NEVER BEEN TO ANYTHING LIKE THAT. I'VE NEVER BEEN TO A WAKE OR A FUNERAL OR ANYTHING.

ME NEITHER.

WHAT DO PEOPLE DO AT A MEMORIAL SERVICE?

I DUNNO...

BUT MOM KEEPS TALKING ABOUT ALL THE **FOOD** THEY'RE GOING TO NEED!

IS EVERYONE'S SUITCASE HERE?

I THINK SO.

I'LL GO UPSTAIRS AND SEE IF GRANDPA NEEDS SOME HELP.

GRANDPA?... YOUR ROOM LOOKS AWFULLY BARE.

I KNOW. I'VE BEEN PACKING UP MY MEMENTOS, MICHAEL.

I'M GOING HOME.

WELL, IT LOOKS AS THOUGH THE YOUNG COUSINS HAVE PICKED UP WHERE THEY LEFT OFF!

YES, THEY'RE HAVING A GREAT TIME TOGETHER.

THEY MUST FORGET THEY'RE RELATED!

MORE THAN 60 PEOPLE ARE COMING TO AUNT MARIAN'S FAREWELL, ELLY.

THOSE WHO AREN'T BILLETED WITH FAMILY ARE STAYING AT THE RIVERSIDE INN.

THE SERVICE WILL BE AT THE BOTANICAL GARDENS AND THE RECEPTION AT THE MASONIC HALL. MUSIC AND FLOWERS AND REFRESHMENTS ARE TAKEN CARE OF.

THIS DOESN'T SOUND LIKE A MEMORIAL SERVICE—IT SOUNDS MORE LIKE A CELEBRATION!

.....IT IS.

WHERE ARE YOU GOING, LIZARDBREATH?

TO PRACTICE WITH UNCLE PHIL.

I HAVE TO SING FOR GRANDMA TOMORROW, AND HE'S GOING TO PLAY THE GUITAR.

I THOUGHT YOU WERE GOING TO SING ACAPPELLA.

I WAS, BUT THIS IS BETTER.

WHAT DOES ACAPPELLA MEAN?

....OFF KEY.

MICHAEL, HOWCOME A STONE CAN SKIP ACROSS THE WATER LIKE THAT?

BECAUSE IT HAS A FLAT BOTTOM

ANYTHING THAT'S SMALL AND HEAVY AND HAS A FLAT BOTTOM CAN SKIP ACROSS THE WATER.

BRRRR

AAAAHHHHHH

SPLASH

YOU KNOW ME, SIS.... I JUST HATE TO SEE ANYONE SUFFER!

THIS IS A GREAT BEACH!

YEAH. MOM USED TO COME HERE ALL THE TIME WHEN SHE WAS A KID.

WHY DID SHE EVER LEAVE?

SHE WENT TO UNIVERSITY IN TORONTO, GOT MARRIED — AN' THAT WAS THAT!

BESIDES, IF SHE'D STAYED HERE, SHE NEVER WOULD HAVE MET DAD, AN' IF SHE NEVER MET DAD, WE WOULDN'T BE **HERE**!

OH.

WHAT DID **DAD** HAVE TO DO WITH IT?

I'M GLAD MOM LET US TAKE OFF BY OURSELVES.

YEAH. WE DON'T GET TO DO THIS TOO OFTEN.

WHAT'S HAPPENING WITH YOU, MIKE? I MEAN, REALLY.

I DUNNO, SIS. I'M IN A STATE OF CONFUSION.

SOMETIMES I'M SURE ABOUT WHAT I WANT TO DO AND WHERE I WANT TO GO—BUT AT THIS MOMENT...I HAVEN'T GOT A CLUE!

ARE YOU STILL SEEING DEANNA?

EVERY TIME I SHUT MY EYES.

IT'S WIERD ABOUT DEANNA, SIS. I KNOW SHE LOVES ME. SHE'S NOT INTERESTED IN ANYONE ELSE.

SHE JUST DOESN'T WANT TO MAKE A COMMITMENT.

WHY DO YOU WANT A COMMITMENT? YOU'RE NOT READY TO GET MARRIED!

YOU'VE GOT THE REST OF YOUR LIFE AHEAD OF YOU.

I KNOW.

AND, I WANT TO SPEND IT WITH DEANNA.

MICHAEL, LOOK!—I'VE GOT **CRABS!**

S'IL VOUS PLAIT

SEE? IF YOU TURN OVER ONE OF THESE ROCKS, YOU'LL FIND... **HAH!** THERE'S ANOTHER ONE!

I'VE GOT 12 OF THEM, NOW!

THAT'S COOL, APRIL. WHERE ARE YOU KEEPING THE OTHERS?

SO I'VE TOLD YOU ABOUT DEANNA, LIZ. WHAT'S WITH YOU? STILL GOING WITH ANTHONY?

YEAH.

HE'S A REALLY NICE GUY AN' EVERYTHING—BUT I DON'T THINK IT'S, YOU KNOW... FOREVER.

WELL, OF COURSE IT'S NOT FOREVER!—HE'S YOUR FIRST LOVE! FIRST LOVE ISN'T EVEN LOVE!

OH? WHAT DO YOU CALL IT, THEN?

... PRACTICE.

YOU ARE SO FULL OF IT, MICHAEL. MARTHA WAS THE FIRST GIRL YOU DATED, AND YOU WERE CRAZY ABOUT HER. YOU CALLED IT LOVE!

OH, COME ON, LIZ!!

YOU'RE SAYING THAT WHEN KIDS FALL IN LOVE, IT'S NOT LOVE.

IT'S PUPPY LOVE!

NO MATTER WHAT YOU CALL IT, LOVE IS LOVE UNTIL IT'S OVER.

HOW DID YOU GET SO SMART?

..... I'VE BEEN IN LOVE A FEW TIMES.

IT WAS A BEAUTIFUL RECEPTION, ELLY—AND THE MEMORIAL SERVICE WAS LOVELY.

WHAT HAPPENED TO THE KIDS?

THEY WERE GETTING BORED, SO DAD SENT THEM OFF TO THE BEACH.

REALLY? WITH DOZENS OF RELATIVES HERE? I CAN'T IMAGINE HOW ANYONE COULD POSSIBLY BE BORED!

WELL, DAD, IT'S OVER. WHAT HAPPENS NOW?

I STILL HAVE A LOT OF PAPERWORK TO DO... AND YOUR MOTHER'S THINGS TO GO THROUGH.

ARE YOU READY FOR THAT?

YES. I'M STARTING TO HEAL, ELLY. IT'S THE STRANGEST THINGS THAT LET YOU KNOW.

WE SHARED A BED FOR OVER 50 YEARS...

THIS SIDE WAS HER SIDE—THAT SIDE WAS MINE.

LAST NIGHT.... I SLEPT IN THE MIDDLE.

HI, AUNTIE CHERYL—WE'RE BACK!—WHERE'S MOM?

SHE'S STILL AT YOUR GRANDPA'S. DID YOU HAVE FUN AT THE BEACH?

YAH!—LOOKIT I GOT!

YECCH!—THAT BELONGS UNDER A ROCK SOMEWHERE. GET IT OUT OF THE HOUSE!

CATS AND KIDS! THEY ALWAYS BRING HOME THE MOST **DISGUSTING** THINGS!

I KNEW THERE WAS A REASON WHY I LIKED YOU!!

AUNTIE ELLY! COME AN' SEE WHAT WE MADE!!

IT'S A ZOO, SEE? THERE'S ANTS, A BEE, A WORM, A SPIDER A GARDEN SNAKE, AN' APRIL GOT A CRAB FROM THE BEACH!

DON'T WORRY. WE'RE GONNA LET THEM ALL GO.

I'M GLAD TO HEAR IT.

WE'VE HAD SUCH A NICE TIME, CHERYL. THANKS FOR PUTTING US ALL UP.

IT WAS FUN, WASN'T IT?

IT WAS A PERFECT VISIT.

JUST LONG ENOUGH.

THE ADULTS ARE STARTING TO FIDGET...

JINGLE JINGLE

AND THE KIDS ARE STARTING TO FIGHT.

DAD, ARE YOU SURE YOU DON'T WANT TO COME BACK TO ONTARIO WITH US?

I'M SURE, DEAR. AT LEAST FOR NOW.

MY HOUSE IS HERE, OUR FRIENDS ARE HERE, YOUR MOTHER IS BURIED HERE. THIS IS WHERE I BELONG.

BESIDES, YOU HAVE YOUR OWN LIVES TO LEAD. YOU DON'T NEED ME HANGING AROUND, GETTING IN THE WAY.

YOU WERE NEVER IN THE WAY, DAD.

... YOU WERE ALWAYS IN THE BATHROOM!

WE'RE GOING TO MISS YOU, GRANDPA.

I'LL MISS YOU TOO, APRIL.

BUT YOU KNOW WHAT? YOU TAUGHT ME SOMETHING WHILE I WAS STAYING AT YOUR HOUSE.

I DID?

I FOUND OUT THAT I NEED A LIVE-IN COMPANION.

YOU'RE GOING TO GET A ROOM-MATE?

.... I'M GOING TO GET A DOG.

ELLY, WHY DON'T YOU JUST PUT ON YOUR GLASSES?

SHE DOESN'T WANT PEOPLE TO KNOW SHE NEEDS THEM!!

GOODBYE, DAD. I'LL SEE YOU AT CHRISTMAS.

THANKS FOR EVERYTHING, CHERYL.

ANY TIME, JOHN.

I'LL CALL YOU WHEN WE GET HOME, SIS.

SAYING GOODBYE IS SURE A LOT EASIER FOR BIG PEOPLE!

YOU GET TO HUG THE TOP HALF!!

KNOW WHAT, DAD? I THOUGHT IT WAS GONNA BE A DRAG BEING AROUND RELATIVES FOR A WEEK.

- WITH ALL OF THEM SAYING, "LOOK HOW GROWN-UP YOU ARE!" AN' STUFF LIKE THAT.

BUT THEY WERE PRETTY COOL! ...I WAS WONDERING WHY I FELT OK ABOUT THEM THIS TIME.

PROBABLY BECAUSE OF HOW GROWN-UP YOU ARE!

YOU'RE SO QUIET, MOM. ARE YOU THINKING ABOUT GRANDMA MARIAN?

UH-HUH.

SHE WAS A KIND PERSON WHO LED AN INTERESTING LIFE. I WAS THINKING THAT HER MEMORIAL SERVICE WAS LIKE THE ENDING TO A GOOD NOVEL.

I GUESS EVERYONE'S LIFE IS LIKE A NOVEL. SOME OF IT IS WRITTEN BY FATE, SOME OF IT IS WRITTEN BY GOD.

I AGREE...

...BUT THE PART WE ARE ULTIMATELY JUDGED BY IS THE PART WE WRITE OURSELVES.

THE DINNER I'M GOING TO STARTS AT 6, JOHN, SO I'VE PREPARED EVERYTHING FOR YOU HERE.

THERE'S A NICE CASSE-ROLE IN THE FRIDGE JUST PUT IT IN THE MICROWAVE AND THEN INTO THE OVEN AT 350° 'TIL IT BUBBLES...

PUT FROZEN PEAS INTO A COVERED PYREX DISH AND MICROWAVE ON HIGH FOR 3 MINUTES, STIR AND HEAT AGAIN...

I BOUGHT BUNS, THERE'S A FRESH GARDEN SALAD AND FOR DESSERT, THERE'S... WE'LL BE FINE, MOM-HONEST!!

BURGORAMA DOGORAMA SPUDZORAMA!!

123

124

HEY, GORDO!

MIKE! WE HEARD YOU WERE BACK. —IT'S GOOD TO SEE YOU!

SO, WHAT'S HAPPENING?

A LOT, ACTUALLY. WE'RE GOING TO ADD ANOTHER WORK BAY TO THE GARAGE AND A COFFEE SHOP!

BUT, THE BIG NEWS IS— WE'RE GOING TO HAVE ANOTHER BABY!

REALLY? CONGRATULATIONS!!

TRACEY!—I HEAR YOU'RE EXPANDING!!!

ANOTHER BABY!—DOES MY MOM KNOW?

NOT YET. YOU WERE ALL IN VANCOUVER WHEN WE GOT THE NEWS.

PAUL'S OLD ENOUGH TO FEED AND AMUSE HIMSELF NOW, SO WE THOUGHT IT WAS TIME.

MAN, A BIG BUSINESS AND TWO KIDS?—AND, HERE I AM STILL FLOUNDERING AROUND IN SCHOOL! —COMPARED TO YOU GUYS, I'VE GOT NOTHING!

MIKE ... ENJOY IT WHILE YOU CAN.

SO, THIS END HERE WILL BE A COFFEE SHOP!

JUST A SMALL ONE. FOUR TABLES AND A COUNTER.

WE GET SO MUCH TRAFFIC THROUGH HERE, AND WE ALREADY SELL POP, COFFEE AND SANDWICHES, SO....

GORD, WHEN YOU BOUGHT THIS PLACE, DID YOU EVER EXPECT IT WOULD BECOME SUCH A SUCCESS?

I DUNNO!

BUT YOU DON'T WORK THIS HARD TO BECOME A FAILURE!

HOW ARE YOU GOING TO MANAGE ANOTHER BABY IN THIS TINY APARTMENT?!

WELL, THAT'S ANOTHER STORY.

TRACEY'S PARENTS BOUGHT A CONDO, SO WE'RE RENTING OUR APARTMENT TO ONE OF OUR MECHANICS, AND MOVING TO THEIR HOUSE!

WAIT. TOO MUCH IS HAPPENING HERE! - YOU'VE GOT A HOUSE? ... NEXT YOU'RE GOING TO TELL ME YOUR HAIR'S GOING GREY!

IT'S NOT GOING GREY, MIKE ..... IT'S JUST GOING!

SO, TELL US ABOUT YOU!

I DON'T HAVE A LOT TO TELL YOU, GORD. I GO BACK TO UNIVERSITY IN SEPTEMBER

I'VE BEEN WORKING ON A PROJECT WITH MY ROOMMATE AND...

SO! HOW'S DEANNA?

ELIZABETH TOLD US YOU'RE PRETTY SERIOUS ABOUT HER. IS IT TRUE, MIKE? ARE YOU GOING TO "POP THE QUESTION?"

... I'M GOING TO "POP" ELIZABETH.

TRACEY, IF ELIZABETH TOLD YOU I WAS THINKING ABOUT GETTING MARRIED, SHE WAS WRONG.

DEANNA AND I DON'T GRADUATE FOR ANOTHER YEAR, THEN WE'LL HAVE STUDENT LOANS TO PAY OFF—AND WHO KNOWS WHERE WE'LL BE LIVING BY THEN!

MARRIED?! HAH!!! THAT IS ABSOLUTELY THE FARTHEST THING FROM MY MIND! - I'M NOT PLANNING TO GET MARRIED!

ENGAGED THEN?

MAYBE.

127